MILITARY MISSIONS

RESCUE

BY NEL YOMTOV

BELLWETHER MEDIA • MINNEAPOLIS, MN

EPIC

EPIC BOOKS are no ordinary books. They burst with intense action, high-speed heroics, and shadows of the unknown. Are you ready for an Epic adventure?

This edition first published in 2017 by Bellwether Media, Inc.

No part of this publication may be reproduced in whole or in part without written permission of the publisher.
For information regarding permission, write to Bellwether Media, Inc., Attention: Permissions Department, 5357 Penn Avenue South, Minneapolis, MN 55419.

Library of Congress Cataloging-in-Publication Data

Names: Yomtov, Nelson, author.
Title: Rescue / by Nel Yomtov.
Description: Minneapolis, MN : Bellwether Media, Inc., 2017. | Series: Epic: Military Missions | Includes bibliographical references and index. | Audience: Grades 2-7.
Identifiers: LCCN 2016006235 | ISBN 9781626174382 (hardcover : alk. paper)
Subjects: LCSH: Search and rescue operations–United States–Juvenile literature. | United States–Armed Forces–Search and rescue operations–Juvenile literature.
Classification: LCC U167.5.S32 Y67 2017 | DDC 355.4/1–dc23
LC record available at http://lccn.loc.gov/2016006235

Printed in the United States of America, North Mankato, MN.

TABLE OF CONTENTS

RESCUE AT SEA

A storm crashes into a small fishing boat. The crew is in trouble! Big waves knock them into the water. Luckily, help is on the way.

A team from the United States Coast Guard races to the scene in a **motorboat**. Members of the team jump into the water. They guide the crew to safety.

SAVING LIVES
The Coast Guard saves about 10 lives each day!

THE MISSION

Every branch of the U.S. military carries out rescue missions. Teams rescue both soldiers and **civilians**. In war, teams rescue troops in enemy **territory**. The soldiers may be hurt or trapped by the enemy.

civilian rescue

soldier rescue

9

Civilians are rescued for many reasons. Rescue teams help people during **natural disasters** like floods and **earthquakes**. The teams also save lives during dangerous events like fires.

REAL-LIFE RESCUE

What: Rescue mission to save two people from a band of pirates

Who: U.S. Navy SEAL Team Six

Where: Somalia, Africa

When: January 25, 2012

Why: Rescue aid workers taken hostage

How: SEAL Team Six landed from a plane near the pirates' base in Somalia; attacked pirate base and successfully rescued Poul Thisted and Jessica Buchanan.

Poul Thisted

Jessica Buchanan

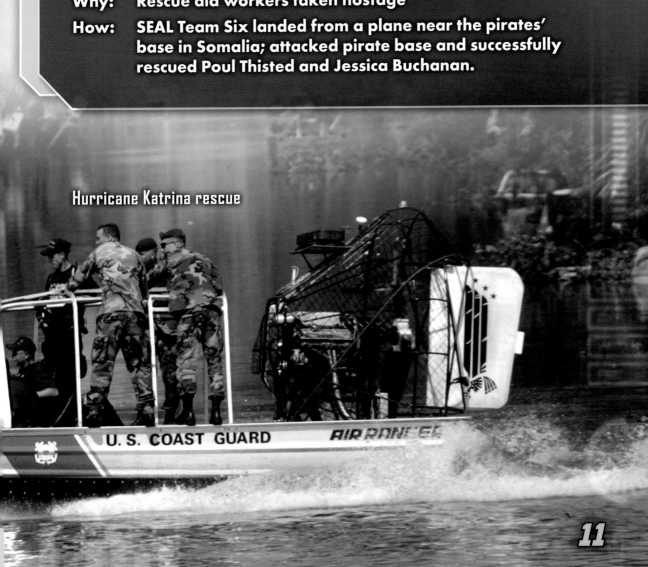

Hurricane Katrina rescue

U.S. COAST GUARD   AIR RANGER

THE PLAN

Rescue missions use special supplies and materials. Soldiers carry different types of weapons.

They often use helicopters and planes. Fast motorboats help rescue people at sea.

The U.S. military also uses dogs and robots in rescue missions. Specially trained dogs sniff out people in danger. Rescue robots find people trapped in fallen buildings or mine accidents.

RESCUE EQUIPMENT AND GEAR

M4 carbine

M9 pistol

Coast Guard MLB
(motor lifeboat)

Jayhawk
helicopter

THE TEAM

The U.S. Navy, Air Force, and Coast Guard rescue people from the water. They help **airmen** and others lost at sea.

U.S. Air Force
pararescueman

PJs TO THE RESCUE

The Air Force rescue team is the Special Operations Command. Team members are called pararescuemen, or PJs.

The Army and Marines work on both land and water.

Members of rescue teams are specially trained. They learn how to **parachute** from aircraft. They also learn swimming skills.

Team members are even taught how to care for sick and hurt people.

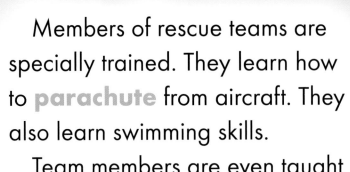

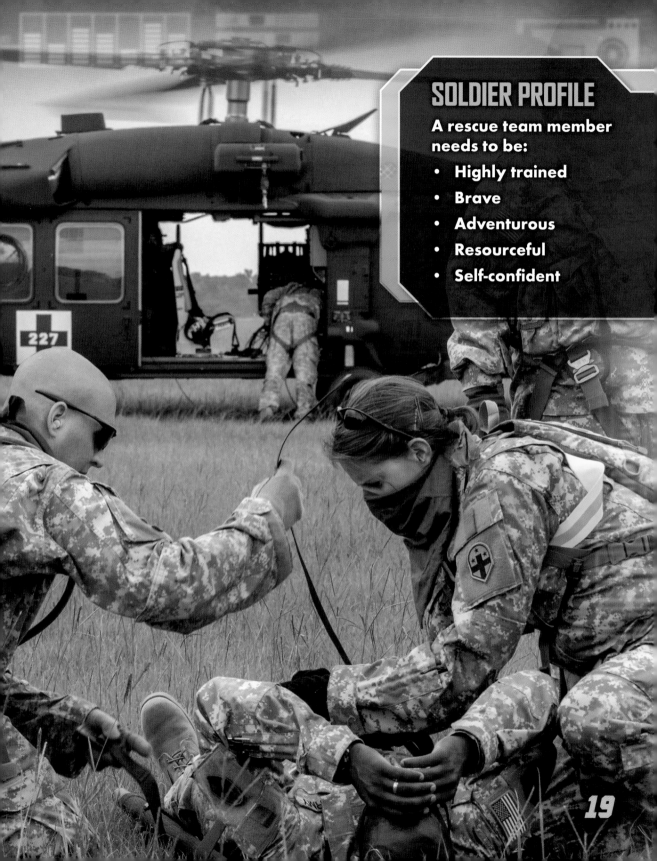

A rescue team member needs to be:
- **Highly trained**
- **Brave**
- **Adventurous**
- **Resourceful**
- **Self-confident**

227

ACCOMPLISHED!

Rescue missions save lives and return people to safety. When a mission ends, the team prepares for its next job.

Rescue teams must be ready for action at all times.

GLOSSARY

airmen—members of the crew of an aircraft, especially in an air force

civilians—people who are not members of the armed forces or a police force

earthquakes—sudden, violent shakings of the earth that may damage buildings and injure people

motorboat—a small boat with an engine

natural disasters—natural events that cause great damage; floods, hurricanes, and earthquakes are a few natural disasters.

parachute—to jump from an aircraft with a parachute; a parachute is a large, umbrella-shaped cloth attached to someone to help them fall safely from the air.

territory—an area of land owned by a group or a government

TO LEARN MORE

AT THE LIBRARY

Markovics, Joyce. *Today's Coast Guard Heroes*. New York, N.Y.: Bearport Pub., 2012.

McDonnell, Julia. *Coast Guard*. New York, N.Y.: Gareth Stevens Pub., 2012.

Slater, Lee. *Pararescue Jumpers*. Minneapolis, Minn.: ABDO Publishing, 2016.

ON THE WEB

Learning more about rescue is as easy as 1, 2, 3.

1. Go to www.factsurfer.com.

2. Enter "rescue" into the search box.

3. Click the "Surf" button and you will see a list of related web sites.

With factsurfer.com, finding more information is just a click away.

INDEX

The images in this book are reproduced through the courtesy of: Przemek Tokar, front cover (left); Oleg Zabielin, front cover (top right); United States Department of Defense/ DVIDS, front cover (bottom right), pp. 4, 5, 5 (top), 6-7, 7, 9, 12, 13, 13 (top), 14, 14 (top), 15 (middle right), 16, 17, 18, 18 (top), 20, 21; David J. Phillip/ AP Images, p. 8; Menahem Kahana/ AFP/ Getty Images, pp. 10-11; Danish Refugee Council/ ZUMA Press, p. 11 (top right, top left); Militarist, p. 15 (top); Jaroslaw Grudzinski, p. 15 (middle left); Phil Lowe, p. 15 (bottom); XM Collection/ Alamy, pp. 18-19.